The Opossum at Night

by Anne O'Brien
illustrated by Deborah Colvin Borgo

Core Decodable 79

McGraw Hill Education

Bothell, WA • Chicago, IL • Columbus, OH • New York, NY

MHEonline.com

Send all inquiries to:
McGraw-Hill Education
8787 Orion Place
Columbus, OH 43240

ISBN: 978-0-02-132192-6
MHID: 0-02-132192-2

Printed in the United States of America.

10 11 12 13 KOD 24

Opossums do not like the light.
Daytime is bright.
An opossum sees better at night.

When it is night, an opossum wakes.
She hunts for insects to feed her babies.

A dog frightens the opossum.
The opossum freezes.
She stays still and plays dead.

Night is over. It begins to get light.

The opossum returns to her tree.
Her babies wait for her.

It is time for sleep.
The opossum stays with her babies.
They might play later at night.